IMAGES
of America

HIGH POINT STATE PARK
AND THE
CIVILIAN CONSERVATION CORPS

CURRENT
CAMP CAPERS

THE LIBR
AUG
UNIVERSITY

VOL. 3 NO. 18 COMPANY 1280 SUSSEX, N.J. JULY 1939

HIGH POINT MONUMENT
FROM
LAKE MARCIA

When the Civilian Conservation Corps left High Point State Park in 1941, it left a legacy of hard work, attractive design, and excellent construction. We tip our hats to Pres. Franklin D. Roosevelt, whose vision for a CCC came to fruition, and to the men and women of the National Park Service, War Department, and Department of Labor, and the young men who all made it possible. To them we offer our collective thanks. (Courtesy Center for Research Libraries Collection.)

IMAGES
of America

HIGH POINT STATE PARK
AND THE
CIVILIAN CONSERVATION CORPS

Peter Osborne

ARCADIA
PUBLISHING

Copyright © 2002 by Minisink Valley Historical Society
ISBN 978-0-7385-1084-2

Published by Arcadia Publishing
Charleston, South Carolina

Printed in the United States of America

Library of Congress Catalog Card Number: 2002108403

For all general information, contact Arcadia Publishing:
Telephone 843-853-2070
Fax 843-853-0044
E-mail sales@arcadiapublishing.com
For customer service and orders:
Toll-free 1-888-313-2665

Visit us on the Internet at www.arcadiapublishing.com

Dedicated to my wife, Janis.

(Reprinted from *We Can Take It:
A Short Story of the CCC*.)

CONTENTS

ACKNOWLEDGMENTS

Without the following people, institutions, and agencies, I could not have completed this book, which remembers and honors the fine work of the men of the Civilian Conservation Corps (CCC) who were at High Point State Park. First, I must acknowledge my wife, Janis, who edited the copy, helped select photographs, and was as supportive as always. I am in the debt of John Keator, superintendent of High Point State Park, who was always gracious and helpful, allowed access to the park's archives, and read the manuscript. His staff was equally helpful and patient. They include Carol J. Forbes, Renee Bonham, Philip Fancher, and Kate Monahan, who also read the manuscript and provided many necessary corrections. The majority of the photographs are from the park's collection, and I am grateful to the park for allowing me to use them. The Friends of High Point allowed access to the park's large collection of photographs and let me borrow them for an extended period. Myra Snook and Roberta Bramhall were helpful in sorting through the large collection and assisting me in my quest for information.

I am especially grateful to regional historian Ronald Dupont Jr. for his assistance and sharing of knowledge over the years and for reading this manuscript. His extensive research and writings on High Point form the basis of our knowledge of the park's history. Ron also allowed for the reprinting of an 1845 road map of the High Point area, which is included.

William Wurst and Debbie Fritter conducted a series of interviews with former CCC boys that provided insight into the photographs in this book. Those CCC boys and former National Park Service employees provided a great deal of information in identifying photographs. They include Albert Mastriani, Peter Lutz, Michael Sagursky, "Red" Sacco, Thomas Segar, Neil Thiede, and Nicholas Hanisak. All were generous with their time and insights into the CCC's operation at High Point.

Barbara Sagursky Pohl, daughter of enrollee Michael Sagursky, donated photographs, as did Jane Gibbons Proctor, daughter of John Gibbons, Myra Snook, and Robert Quinn. Leslie Crine was kind enough to take photographs that filled in some of the blank spots. Basil Nickerson kindly gave permission to use previously copyrighted materials. James Simon from the Center for Research Libraries in Chicago assisted me in getting the High Point camp newsletters. The illustrations from the camp newsletters are reproduced from CCC Camp Papers held by the Center for Research Libraries, and for their permission to use them we are grateful.

My board of directors at the Minisink Valley Historical Society (MVHS) in Port Jervis allowed me to work on the project and bring it to fruition. Kelly Millspaugh, an intern at MVHS, transcribed audio tapes of former CCC boys recorded at High Point over the years, which provided a great deal of information. Society member Margie Sierski assisted greatly with research by reading many reels of newspaper microfilms. Bill Clark, Nancy Bello, Nancy Conod, Nancy Vocci, Les and Jean Crine, Irene Cosh, Stella Kelsch, Charles King, Miral Haubner, Susan Stanton, Kevin Smith, and Bill Bavoso all provided help. Mary and Mead Stapler offered encouragement and invaluable assistance.

The following people all provided additional information: the staff and members of the National Association of Civilian Conservation Corps Alumni; Julie Kemper; Joe Toltin; the Brotherhood of XCCCers; the staff of the Port Jervis Free Library; RoseMary Conklin, St. Mary's Church, Port Jervis, New York; Wayne McCabe; Alicia Batko; Montague Association for the Restoration of Community History; Robert Longcore, Sussex County Historical Society; Steve Bates, the Nature Conservancy; Trailblazers Camp; Len Peck, Walpack Historical Society; Donald Eby; Florence Fuller; Lois and Andy Fortune; Walter Gochenour; Helen Cuddeback; Pat Governale; Frank Toth; Paul Lighty; Gerald Tomlinson; Florence Gray; Dick Heiney, Promised Land State Park, Greentown, Pennsylvania; Sandra Schultz, acting superintendent, National Park Service, Upper Delaware Scenic and Recreation River; Helen Connelly; Ann Marino; and Zita Innella.

INTRODUCTION

This is a book about two important developments in New Jersey history: first, the creation of one of the state's most famous parks, and second, the progression of the largest conservation initiative ever undertaken in New Jersey and nationwide. It is a story of grand generosity, a beautiful monument, and the realization of a president's vision, the legacy of which lives on some 70 years later.

The first part of this story concerns a gift of land that created High Point State Park and reflects the generosity of Col. Anthony Kuser and his wife, Susie Dryden Kuser. The gift was the first of its kind in the state and has not been duplicated since. The establishment of High Point Park was part of a national trend from 1910 to 1940, when a large number of state and national parks and forests were created all across the country. The period has been called the Golden Age of Parks. High Point was among the earliest and most important parks in New Jersey.

The High Point Park Commission, created to manage the park, was unique in the high level of personal, inspirational, and financial support it received from its committee members. The committee members guided the park in its early years and funded, out of their own pockets, a park study by the Olmsted Brothers landscape architectural firm. Although they lived in a time when funding for parks was minimal, committee members managed to acquire revenue from the state to establish many projects that are still in place today.

The second part of this story focuses on the Depression-era federal agency known as the Civilian Conservation Corps (CCC), which was also unprecedented and has yet to be duplicated. The CCC was the brainchild of one of the 20th century's most influential American presidents, Franklin Delano Roosevelt. The agency had two goals: first, to help unemployed young men between the ages of 17 and 24 and veterans of World War I to find work, and second, to initiate thousands of conservation projects across the nation in parks, forests, and at historic sites. From 1933 to 1941, about 2,000 young men worked at High Point in the CCC, under the supervision of the National Park Service and the U.S. Army.

When the CCC boys first arrived at High Point Park, they found a relatively undeveloped 11,000-acre parcel of land. Almost all of the visitors used only the land surrounding Lake Marcia and the Kuser Lodge. Literally thousands of people crammed into this small 100-acre parcel each year. By the time the CCC boys were done working eight years later, they had built 25 miles of roads, two lakes, repaired the badly damaged forest, fought forest fires, cleared trails, built campgrounds and shelters, and partially completed an athletic complex. The park, as visitors enjoy it today, is largely the fruition of their efforts.

This book tells about the operation of the CCC camp and recalls what life was like for a typical enrollee. It also tells the story of how the effort was managed and how projects were completed. Many of the photographs included in the book come from the personal collections of the young men who served at High Point and who are now in their late 70s and 80s. Readers are invited to visit the park and to follow the progress of the work projects through almost 200 photographs.

This is the first book to photographically reveal the history of the single greatest conservation effort ever undertaken at High Point State Park. The roads that provide essential access, the lakes that offer fishermen and boaters a place to enjoy their sports, and the trails that thousands of hikers still use, all built by the CCC, form the basis of visitors' experiences in the park today.

Since 1945, when the state disbanded the High Point Park Commission and incorporated the park into the State Park Service within the Division of Parks and Forestry, High Point has continued to be one of the jewels in the crown of the system. However, High Point, like all of the state's parks and forests, has been affected by budget cuts, a reality that hurts the park and us, the users. After all, they are the people's parks and forests.

One of the purposes of this book is to encourage our government leaders to fund our parks and forests in a more adequate fashion. As you read this book, you will see that the need for a program similar to the CCC still exists, not only for the benefit of young people but also for the survival of our parks and forests, which thrived off the loving care, maintenance, and nurturing the CCC gave them 70 years ago.

—Peter Osborne
Executive Director
Minisink Valley Historical Society

One

HIGH POINT PARK

High Point has always been a focal point for New Jersey inhabitants, from the Native Americans to the state's current residents, because of its panoramic views and impressive location on the Kittatinny Ridge. During much of the 19th century, it was the location of hardscrabble farms and charcoal-gathering operations and was the destination of an occasional visitor.

The park has a long history, one that includes a great philanthropist, Col. Anthony Kuser, and his wife, Susie Dryden; a park design originally created by the famed landscape firm of the Olmsted Brothers; and the location of one of the most intensive efforts undertaken by the Civilian Conservation Corps (CCC) in the state of New Jersey. Its popularity has endured.

The generosity of the Kuser family did not end with the donation of land. In 1927, Colonel Kuser offered to build a monument at the top of High Point to honor the veterans from New Jersey who had participated in any of the nation's wars to date. The anticipated cost was $500,000, and the design was patterned after the Bunker Hill Monument.

In the far northwestern corner of New Jersey lies a monument that can be seen from three surrounding states. It stands on the highest point, 1,803 feet above sea level, and is located in High Point State Park. Now covering almost 15,000 acres, the park is one of the largest in the state. (Courtesy Minisink Valley Historical Society.)

In the late 19th century, High Point gained attention when Charles St. John purchased a large tract of land along the ridge, within the present boundaries of the park, and erected a large lodge on it between 1889 and 1890. The lodge was known as the High Point Inn, and its beautiful location and facilities drew visitors from throughout the region. By 1908, the inn closed because of bad economic times and forest fires. (Courtesy Minisink Valley Historical Society.)

Between 1910 and 1919, Col. Anthony Kuser (pictured here) acquired the Charles St. John tract of land, along with other parcels acquired by John Dryden, Kuser's father-in law. In all, the property encompassed about 11,000 acres. Kuser had begun his career as an engineer and had active business interests in brewing, ice, utilities, street railways, automobiles, and motion pictures. Dryden was the founder of the Prudential Insurance Company. (Courtesy Leslie Crine and High Point State Park.)

The Inn, High Point, Sussex, N. J.

Kuser demolished one end of the High Point Inn and turned the remaining portion into a large lodge on the brow of a hill with a spectacular view. It later became known as the Kuser Lodge or the Administration Building. It was used as a hotel beginning in 1937 and later for the park's offices. (Courtesy Minisink Valley Historical Society.)

In 1919, Col. Anthony Kuser offered to sell the lodge to the state, but it declined. In 1923, the Kusers donated the property to the state, and the High Point Park Commission was created to manage the affairs of the park, with John J. Stanton as its first executive secretary. A large crowd came to the opening ceremony to see the park dedicated. (Courtesy Minisink Valley Historical Society.)

STATE OF NEW JERSEY

HIGH POINT PARK

SUSSEX COUNTY

MAP TO ACCOMPANY REPORT OF

OLMSTED BROTHERS – LANDSCAPE ARCHITECTS·

BROOKLINE, MASS. OCTOBER 1923

SCALE 1760' = 1"

LEGEND

PARK BOUNDARY (approximate)

OPENINGS IN FOREST·············

BUILDINGS (existing)·················■ (black)

PARK ROADS & HIGHWAYS OF APPROACH

Once the property was transferred from the Kuser family to the state, the famed Olmsted Brothers landscape architectural firm of Brookline, Massachusetts, was contracted to design the park. The firm supplied the park with a report and large map detailing what could be done with the property. Pictured is the legend from the drawing submitted to the High Point Park Commission. (Courtesy High Point State Park.)

12

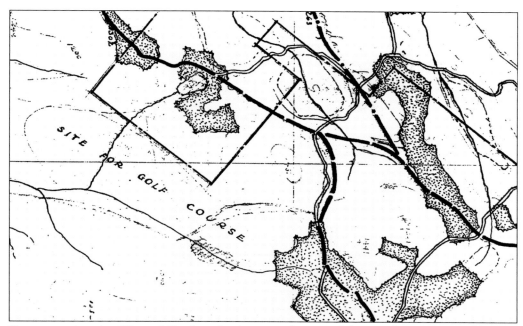

One suggestion the Olmsted Brothers landscape architectural firm made was for a golf course to be built near the summit area on what is now Park Ridge Road, not far from where the Tennessee Gas Pipeline right-of-way is. Park Ridge Road is the dotted line that begins in the lower right corner and travels toward the upper left corner. (Courtesy High Point State Park.)

Another suggestion made by the Olmsted firm was to create a new road to pass through what is now known as the Cedar Swamp, then called Rhododendron Swamp, and along the ridge, arriving at the monument from the north. While this road was partially rebuilt by the CCC, the dotted section was never built, but rather the CCC developed it into the Monument Trail. (Courtesy High Point State Park.)

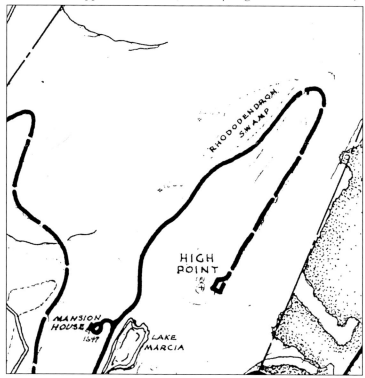

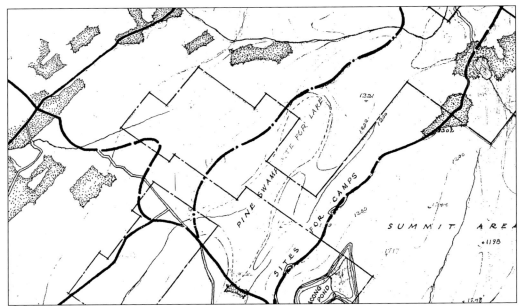

The Olmsted plan also called for a major property acquisition: the expansion of the park to include Mashipacong Pond and the creation of a new lake, adjacent to the pond, in place of a large pine swamp. The road that runs between the two lakes would have been an extension of Park Ridge Road. When the park could not acquire the property, the road was altered and turned east where it passed through the summit area and down to Sawmill Road. (Courtesy High Point State Park.)

In 1927, Col. Anthony Kuser offered to erect a large monument on the highest peak in the state. In 1929, the Hoffman Construction Company of Bernardsville began working on the monument. A track was laid up to the peak, and quarried stone was brought to the location from below. (Courtesy Minisink Valley Historical Society.)

14

July 8, 1929
Elevator -104'

A superstructure was built so stones could be lifted into place as the monument, which would ultimately be 220 feet high, emerged. (Courtesy Minisink Valley Historical Society.)

The monument was completed in 1930. Here, workmen pose beneath the completed structure. Thousands came to the dedication ceremony. Unfortunately, Col. Anthony Kuser did not live to see the monument completed, as he died in 1929. (Courtesy Minisink Valley Historical Society.)

The High Point Monument, designed by New York architects M.S. Wyeth and F.R. King, was dedicated to the veterans of America's wars who were from New Jersey. (Courtesy High Point State Park.)

High Point quickly became a popular destination for people coming from around the tri-state region as the widespread use of the automobile grew. People came to see not only the monument but also the museum and exhibits in the Kuser Lodge. There were also captive bears kept on display for visitors to observe. Today, only wild bears can be found in the park, and it is illegal to feed them. (Courtesy Minisink Valley Historical Society.)

Visitors inundated High Point's campsites around Lake Marcia, the highest lake in New Jersey, during the summer months. Here is a typical campsite at the park, built prior to the arrival of the CCC in 1933. (Courtesy High Point State Park.)

The heavy use of facilities around Lake Marcia by tens of thousands of people in the late 1920s and early 1930s created a "Coney Island" effect, as described later by one National Park Service manager. The public beach, which was on the western shore of the lake at the base of the Kuser Lodge, was packed with visitors each summer. (Courtesy High Point State Park.)

In the 1920s and 1930s, the Girl Scout and Boy Scout movements were spreading across the country. Girl Scouts used a beach on the western side of Lake Marcia, and the Boy Scouts had a camp on the southeastern side of the lake. Here, a rowboat filled with Boy Scouts passes by Girl Scouts, some of whom are watching the action carefully. The park was also the location of a camp for blind children, which was located near today's group camping area. (Courtesy High Point State Park.)

From 1929 to 1951, the Hudson Council of Jersey City operated a Boy Scout camp at Lake Marcia. It was called Kamp Henry Kohl and was located at the southern end of the lake. A large mess hall was located where the current ski center is now and stood until 1994. Pictured here are Scouts leaving on changeover day, when they headed home and a new group arrived. (Courtesy Robert Quinn.)

Stone retaining walls lined the new roads, including Scenic Drive with its magnificent vistas both east and west, and visitors could take in the views at two scenic observatories along the park's eastern border. Today, there is only one observation deck, rebuilt by the Young Adult Conservation Corps in the late 1970s and refurbished by the park in 2000. Existing roads were also improved. (Courtesy Leslie Crine.)

This photograph of the newly constructed comfort station at the northern end of Lake Marcia was taken in October 1934. The station is believed to have been built by the park and is still used by visitors. The large boulders that served as a barrier are now gone. (Courtesy High Point State Park.)

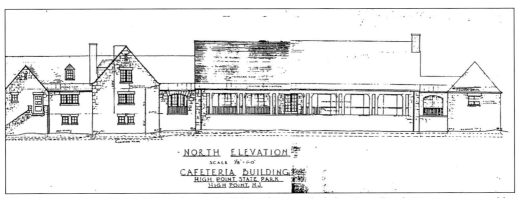

NORTH ELEVATION
SCALE ⅛"=1'-0"
CAFETERIA BUILDING
HIGH POINT STATE PARK
HIGH POINT, N.J.

This elevation drawing of the cafeteria building, later called the Grey Rock Inn, was created by New York architects M.S. Wyeth and F.R. King. Constructed in 1930–1931, the building now serves as the park's Interpretive Center. (Courtesy High Point State Park.)

The stone used for the Grey Rock Inn has a grayish tint and hence the name. The stone also has a reddish tint, reflecting the iron content and creating some confusion about the building's name. The stonework, large timbering, and vaulted ceilings make it one of the most beautiful buildings in the park. (Courtesy High Point State Park.)

This 1939 photograph of the interior of the cafeteria shows why it was such a popular building for use by the public for social affairs, agricultural shows, civic activities, and reunions over the years. (Courtesy High Point State Park.)

Left: John J. Stanton was the first executive secretary (1923–1934) of the High Point Park Commission, and much of his professional life in some way involved the High Point property. He was the owner of the *Sussex Independent* and was a prominent Sussex County resident. (Reprinted from *Northwestern New Jersey: A History of Somerset, Morris, Hunterdon, Warren and Sussex.*) *Right:* Seeley Quince served on the High Point Park Commission, was a prominent Sussex County figure, and played a key role in the park's history. He was the water superintendent, the mayor of Sussex, and owner of a hardware business in the borough. He also served on the county's board of freeholders. (Reprinted from *Northwestern New Jersey: A History of Somerset, Morris, Hunterdon, Warren and Sussex Counties.*)

John Gibbons, the commission's second executive secretary, became the first superintendent of High Point State Park, when it was established in 1945. Gibbons was a significant figure in the history of the park. He came to High Point in 1934, just as the CCC arrived, and was responsible for the oversight of the park's major projects. He lived until 1956. (Courtesy Jane Gibbons Proctor.)

Two

CAMP OPERATIONS

The Great Depression descended on America and lasted from 1929 to 1941 against a backdrop of Americans on the move, enjoying their country's newly created parks and forests. However, the nation's public and private lands had been devastated by years of bad management practices. Because of the huge clouds of dust rolling east from the Midwest and the Plains, the decade became known as the Dirty Thirties. Thousands of banks collapsed, and with that, fortunes and savings accounts disappeared. The stock market plummeted, and the nation witnessed unprecedented poverty. Americans became increasingly desperate and sought action from their leaders.

In the presidential election of 1932, Pres. Herbert Hoover was roundly defeated by New York Gov. Franklin D. Roosevelt. As the new president came into office, he called for a "civilian conservation corps." In March 1933, he directed his cabinet to devise a plan to put young men to work in the nation's parks and forests.

By June 1933, the Civilian Conservation Corps had been created by the Emergency Conservation Work Act. For the first time in American history, four different cabinet agencies, the Departments of Labor, Interior, War, and Agriculture, worked together to manage a program, the CCC, under the guidance of CCC director Robert Fechner. In the first year of the agency's existence, there were 22 camps and 4,000 young men enrolled statewide.

Pres. Franklin D Roosevelt's goal was to assist the hundreds of thousands of young men who were unemployed through no fault of their own. It is estimated that one quarter of the men ages 18 to 25 were unemployed during the Depression, mainly in urban areas. However, the Depression affected all young men whether from farms, cities, or small towns. They became the cardinal concern of the CCC. (Reprinted from *We Can Take It: A Short Story of the CCC*.)

These were times like never before or since, and America was devastated by the economic collapse. City of Port Jervis Mayor Wendell Phillips, on the right, helps unload flour, supplied the Red Cross for distribution to the needy, from an Erie Railroad boxcar in the Port Jervis yards during the 1930s. (Courtesy Minisink Valley Historical Society.)

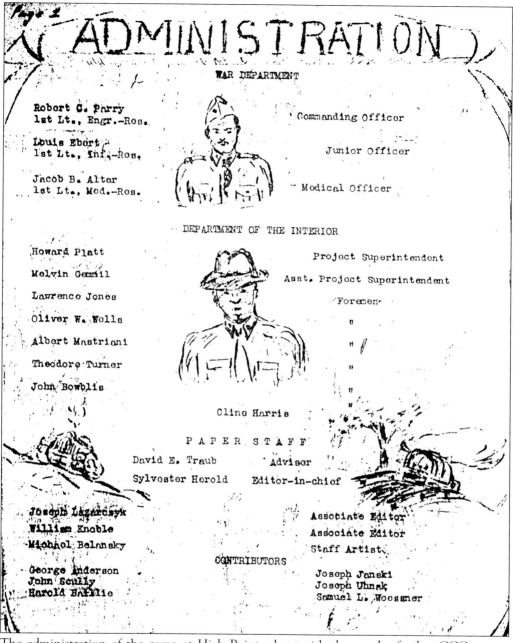

ADMINISTRATION

WAR DEPARTMENT

Robert C. Parry 1st Lt., Engr.-Res.	Commanding Officer
Louis Ebert 1st Lt., Inf.-Res.	Junior Officer
Jacob B. Alter 1st Lt., Med.-Res.	Medical Officer

DEPARTMENT OF THE INTERIOR

Howard Platt	Project Superintendent
Melvin Gemmil	Asst. Project Superintendent
Lawrence Jones	Foremen
Oliver W. Wells	"
Albert Mastriani	"
Theodore Turner	"
John Bowblis	"

Cline Harris

PAPER STAFF

David E. Traub	Advisor
Sylvester Herold	Editor-in-chief
Joseph Lizarczyk	Associate Editor
William Knoble	Associate Editor
Michael Belansky	Staff Artist

CONTRIBUTORS

George Anderson
John Scully
Harold Baillie

Joseph Janski
Joseph Uhnak
Samuel L. Woessner

The administration of the camp at High Point, along with thousands of other CCC camps, was a collaborative effort between the park's executive secretary and the federal Department of Labor, the War Department through the U.S. Army, and in the case of state or national parks, the National Park Service and the U.S. Department of the Interior. Pictured here is an illustration from a camp newsletter showing how the arrangement worked. (Courtesy Center for Research Libraries Collection.)

There were two companies of 200 men each at High Point. Pictured *c.* 1936 or 1937 are Company 216's army officers and National Park Service personnel. In the front row on the right is George O'Neill. In the middle row are, from left to right, an unidentified man, 1st Lt. Clyde Marion, Leigh Saltzman, and Park Service foreman Melvin Gemmill. (Courtesy High Point State Park.)

Pictured is the administration of Company 1280 in the early years of its existence. Second from the left is Oliver Wells, fifth from the left is Albert Mastriani, sixth from the left is Lawrence Jones, and on the far right is Melvin Gemmill. The army essentially ran the camp, overseeing sanitation, food, maintenance, discipline, and payroll. The National Park Service was responsible for work projects. (Courtesy High Point State Park.)

Seated on the running board of this car are four National Park Service foremen. They are, from left to right, Oliver "Nate" Wells, Albert Mastriani, Melvin Gemmill, and Tommy Turner. Foremen received between $150 to $170 per month, and the project superintendent was paid $225 per month. Foremen came from all sorts of backgrounds. Some were college graduates, and others were master craftsmen. (Courtesy High Point State Park.)

In June 1933, the first of what would ultimately be about 2,000 young men arrived at High Point Park to begin their enrollment in CCC Camp No. 2, or Camp Kuser, the second camp created in the state. From June until December, it is believed they lived in a tented camp, pictured here, on the field at the Lusscroft Farm. The camp was located just off Neilson Road in Wantage Township. (Courtesy Myra Snook.)

There are no photographs of the Lusscroft site in the park's archives. This photograph, from the personal collection of Michael Sagursky, shows a typical tented camp that was at either Butler or Newfoundland. The camps were usually placed in open fields, exposing them to the elements and making for difficult living conditions, especially for those men who came from urban environments. (Courtesy Barbara Sagursky Pohl.)

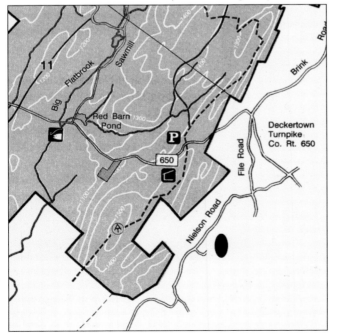

The location of the Lusscroft Farm site is designated on the map by a black oval. There is no evidence as to exactly where the camp was located, although it is believed it was on the field opposite the 4-H camp facilities, facing east. The heavy dark line is the current park boundary, although the park now has jurisdiction over the former 4-H camp. (Courtesy High Point State Park.)

Camp Kuser, the permanent quarters, was built in late 1933 and located at the base of the hill on which the High Point Monument stands. It was a large operation and can be seen in this postcard. Company 216 was located on the lower half of the rows of buildings, and Company 1280 was located on the other side of the street. In all, there were 26 buildings, including recreation halls, an infirmary, shower houses, and maintenance buildings. (Courtesy High Point State Park.)

A large gateway was constructed at the entrance to the camp on Cedar Swamp Drive, and here, Ernie, Bud, and Hurd stand under the sign looking down Company Street. "SP" indicates that it was a state park, and the number indicates the company, which coincided with the Army Corps district. Each company could have as many as 200 men, although that number was not always maintained. (Courtesy High Point State Park.)

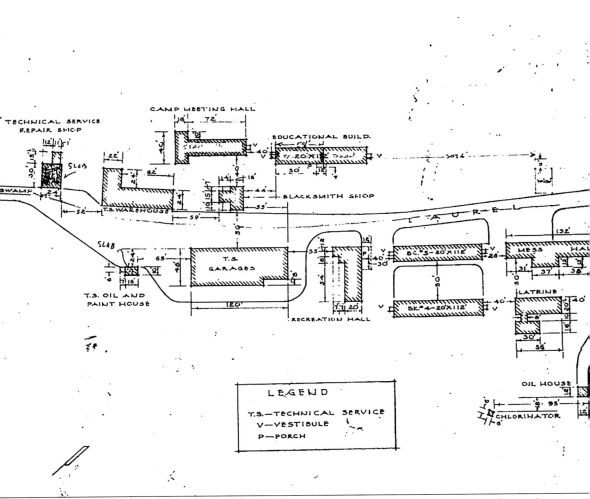

This is the only known drawing of Camp Kuser and dates from 1940. It does not show what the entire camp looked like but does accurately reflect what a typical single company operation was like. Company 1280 occupied the part of the camp pictured here. The camp meeting hall

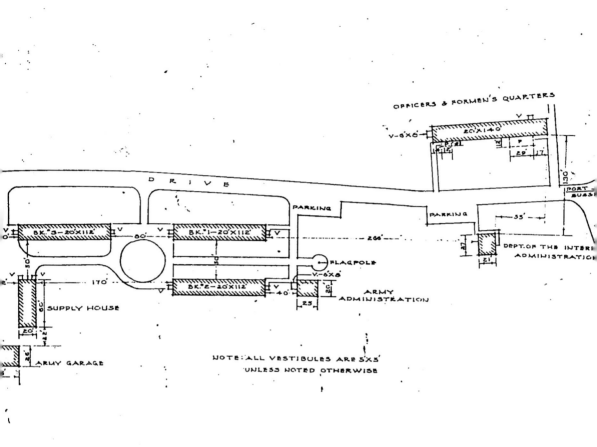

and education building were both former Company 216 buildings, and the remaining barracks buildings for 216 were located directly across the street from the 1280 barracks. (Courtesy High Point State Park.)

This is Barracks 2B in 1937—a typical barracks building at High Point. As part of their compensation, men were provided with room and board. They lived in barracks, which housed about 40 men each, measured 20 feet by 112 feet, and were heated by coal stoves. (Courtesy High Point State Park.)

In this view looking north down Company Street, barracks buildings can be seen on both sides. Enrollees improved the appearance of their barracks by creating walkways, stone borders, and maintaining the buildings. (Courtesy High Point State Park.)

Each man was assigned a bed and a footlocker or closet. Captured here is the interior of Barracks 5, which was at the northern end of the camp and housed enrollees of Company 1280. (Courtesy Barbara Sagursky Pohl.)

Some army officers and National Park Service supervisors who were single or without their families lived full-time at the camp in the officers quarters shown here. Most officers and Park Service supervisors, however, lived in nearby towns like Port Jervis, Milford, and Colesville. (Courtesy High Point State Park.)

Upon arriving at High Point, National Park Service designers working for what was called Technical Services created plans for the development of the 11,000-acre park. First, they made an inventory of what was already in the park. This is a small section of a large drawing illustrating what the area around the monument looked like in the fall of 1933. (Courtesy High Point State Park.)

Foreman Albert Mastriani (left) and National Park Service project superintendent Melvin Gemmill are reviewing plans for work projects at the Park Service office in 1939. Both companies undertook forestry and roadwork projects. In addition, Company 1280 completed most of the construction projects. By 1939, Gemmill had developed an expansive master plan for the park. (Courtesy High Point State Park.)

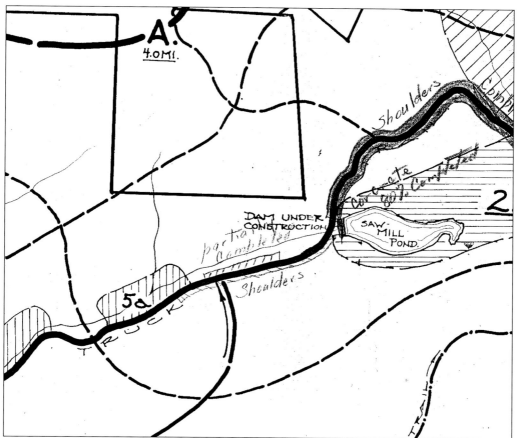

National Park Service designers kept track of finished work projects and issued reports known as progress plans to regional and national offices. Here, the notation indicates that 80 percent of the concrete work on Sawmill Dam is complete, and roadwork along Sawmill Road is continuing. (Courtesy High Point State Park.)

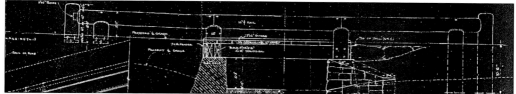

National Park Service designers using style design books, along with their own experience, created working drawings for foremen, which also formed the basis of the progress plans. This cross section for a new bridge construction served as the standard design in the park. (Courtesy High Point State Park.)

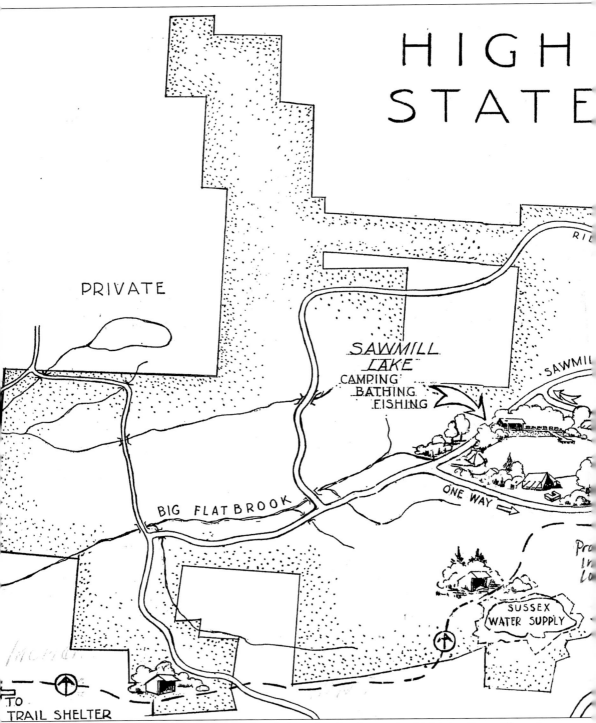

This drawing of High Point State Park is believed to be the work of Melvin Gemmill, project superintendent. After working for the National Park Service, he created some 4,500 illustrations

similar to this one. The drawing probably dates from c.1939 or 1940. (Courtesy High
Point State Park.)

NEW. JERSEY
HIGH POINT PARK COMMISSION

COOPERATING WITH

UNITED STATES

DEPARTMENT OF THE INTERIOR
NATIONAL PARK SERVICE

DRAWN BY A. MASTRIANI	HIGH POINT PARK SHALE·LAKE·PLAY·AREA SEWERAGE SYSTEM FOR LODGE	S.P.-N.J. H.P. 9045-1-1
DESIGNED BY A. MASTRIANI		SCALES AS INDICATED
CHECKED BY M. H. GEMMILL		N.J.S.P.-8 MAY, 15, 1941

PREPARED AND
APPROVED BY _____ _Chas J. Gibbons_ _____ DATE 5/22/41
EXECUTIVE SECRY. HIGH POINT PK. COMM.

RECOMMENDED _____ _Jame H. Burks J._ _____ DATE JUN 11
INSPECTOR

This legend from the Shale Lake Play Area plans demonstrates the cooperative nature of the relationship between the National Park Service and High Point Park Commission, as represented by John Gibbons. Park Service designers Albert Mastriani and Melvin Gemmill prepared the plan, which the High Point Park Commission approved in May 1941. (Courtesy High Point State Park.)

Cooperation between the National Park Service and park staff was excellent. For example, the Park Service staff in Virginia assisted in creating relief maps of the High Point region that were installed in the monument in 1937. It is believed that this photograph was taken of the maps before they were installed. (Courtesy High Point State Park.)

Maintenance buildings were located at the northern end of the camp and housed much of the equipment, including bulldozers, trucks, and graders. (Courtesy High Point State Park.)

Camp Kuser had its own gasoline pump and oil supply, which was located at the northern end. The camp also had its own repair and blacksmith shops for equipment and tools. In the early years, it had its own power generator. (Courtesy High Point State Park.)

The National Park Service provided heavy equipment necessary to undertake the building of dams, roads, and structures. Here, a power shovel with the Park Service label loads two dump trucks from a fill area, probably along Route 23. (Courtesy High Point State Park.)

John "Sharkey" Unangast is at the controls of the National Park Service power shovel. Sharkey was at High Point from 1935 to 1940 and performed much of the excavation work for the dams and lake beds. (Courtesy High Point State Park.)

National Park Service equipment had special license plates designating their ownership by the CCC. On the front of this bulldozer, which is pulling part of a stone crusher, is a license plate that reads, "USCCC 80936 Department of the Interior." (Courtesy High Point State Park.)

A large stone crusher was used to make fill for road and dam projects. The machine is being set up by CCC enrollees at the Steenykill Dam site. The long chain that operated the crushing part of the machinery is probably where an enrollee's pant leg was caught when he was badly injured in 1935. (Courtesy High Point State Park.)

A CCC enrollee drops a rock into a National Park Service stone crusher at the Steenykill Lake construction site to be ground up into smaller material for fill for the dam construction and other park projects. (Courtesy High Point State Park.)

Borrow pits—as the shale quarries at the park were known—provided materials to local road departments since before the CCC's presence up until very recently. Here, CCC boys are setting up a piece of equipment that scoops shale out of a bank and into a crusher. The crushed shale was then loaded into a dump truck. (Courtesy High Point State Park.)

CCC enrollees are shown here working in a local quarry, cutting stone for use in a building project. Until the late 1930s, materials that were drawn from park resources, such as shale and stone, could be used as a credit toward the federal government's expenditures. After that, the park had to absorb some of the expenses for such building materials as concrete. (Courtesy High Point State Park.)

Most materials used for construction projects were taken from the park property itself. What could not be obtained was purchased by the National Park Service. Here, two CCC enrollees work loose a layer of rock for construction projects at Shale Lake. Note the holes already drilled. (Courtesy High Point State Park.)

Safety was an overriding concern in the CCC, reflected in this man's equipment. He is wearing goggles to prevent eye injuries and is using the proper stance while cutting stone. No fatalities ever occurred during the CCC era at High Point, and only one serious accident occurred, when a young man lost an eye while cutting stone and not wearing goggles. (Courtesy High Point State Park.)

Enrollees gathered in front of the Department of the Interior garages every morning at 8:00 a.m. to receive their work assignments where they worked until 4:00 p.m. The men rode in stake body trucks. (Courtesy High Point State Park.)

Form 10—285

UNITED STATES DEPARTMENT OF THE INTERIOR
NATIONAL PARK SERVICE

MOTOR VEHICLE OPERATOR'S PERMIT

NO. _119_ ISSUED _9/21/39_ EXPIRES _12/31/39_

THIS PERMIT, WHEN OFFICIALLY APPROVED AND DATED, AUTHORIZES THE UNDERSIGNED TO OPERATE U.S.D.I. NO. _____ OR ANY MOTOR VEHICLE IN

HIGH POINT PARK
(NAME OF PARK OR MONUMENT)

(signature)
(SIGNATURE OF ISSUING OFFICER)
HOWARD PLATT
Proj. Superintendent
(TITLE)

(signature)
(SIGNATURE OF OPERATOR)
Nat'l Park Service
(ORGANIZATION)
CCC Camp NJ SP-8
Sussex, (New) Jersey

Any violation of Motor Transportation regulations or conviction by any court will be cause for requiring surrender of this permit.

G P O   6—8503

A motor vehicle operator's permit was a valuable item for enrollees to obtain. Not only did it keep them from some of the more unpleasant chores in camp, such as kitchen policing, it was a valuable asset when they left the CCC and went back into the private sector. (Courtesy High Point State Park.)

Here, a CCC truck lies overturned on state Route 23 in 1938. The driver probably lost his rating over this accident. This accident occurred on the first sharp turn going north on Route 23, after the Steenykill Lake entrance. The old roadway can still be seen on the eastern side of the highway. Notice how narrow Route 23 was, barely a two-lane highway. Today, it is three lanes wide with generous shoulders in most places. (Courtesy High Point State Park.)

Three

A DAY IN THE CCC AT CAMP KUSER

While many former CCC boys describe life in camp as similar to being in the military, Pres. Franklin D. Roosevelt made sure that it was not and assured America that it was not. Despite the fact that the camps were run by army officers until the last year or so, the men had much more freedom than if they had been in the military. They were not required to salute officers nor do any military training. The CCC provided room and board, healthcare, clothing, two weeks of vacation, and several holidays. When an enrollee's time was served, he was given transportation back to his hometown.

Most CCC boys remember both the excellent quality and quantity of the food in camp and admit to adopting healthy lifelong eating habits as a result. The men also remember their nights out when they pursued young ladies in the surrounding towns of Port Jervis, Milford, Sussex, and Ogdensburg, and drank nickel beers in local bars that were willing to serve them. For many of the men, their time in the CCC was a great adventure. Of course, some did not enjoy the CCC, but they usually left after a short time. The majority of enrollees found their experiences helped them get ready for a new life when they returned to their homes a little older, wiser, and better trained.

When a new enrollee came into a CCC camp, he was known as a rookie. Rookies were often the subject of pranks played by the more experienced boys. Soon enough they too were playing pranks on newcomers. (Reprinted from *We Can Take It: A Short Story of the* CCC.)

There were some enrollees who shirked their duties and were known as "goldbrickers." They were assigned some of the more unpleasant tasks in camp. If a boy left the CCC without permission, it was said that he had gone "over the hill." If he had served his full term and worked well, he was given an honorable discharge. (Reprinted from *We Can Take It: A Short Story of the* CCC.)

Hearty, healthy food was served at CCC camps. On average, an enrollee gained between 10 and 15 pounds. Pictured here is the interior of the mess hall of Company 1280 at Camp Kuser, where breakfast and dinner were served. (Courtesy High Point State Park.)

Some CCC boys eat their lunch outdoors at Sawmill Dam. Lunch was usually served at the job site, and if big construction projects required round-the-clock work, breakfast and dinner were served there as well. (Courtesy High Point State Park.)

Typically, lunch consisted of a sandwich, fruit, and something to drink. Enterprising lads started a fire to toast their bread or warm their meals. During cold weather, hot lunches were served. (Courtesy High Point State Park.)

The PX (post exchange), or canteen, at High Point was where enrollees bought necessities, as well as candy, cigarettes, postcards, albums, and film. Profits were used to benefit the camp's recreation programs. (Courtesy High Point State Park.)

Medical care was available at all times and provided at no charge. For several years, a doctor was at High Point full-time and in later years, while not on-site, one was readily available. The infirmary at High Point was fully stocked and manned by a senior enrollee who could handle minor medical problems. (Courtesy High Point State Park.)

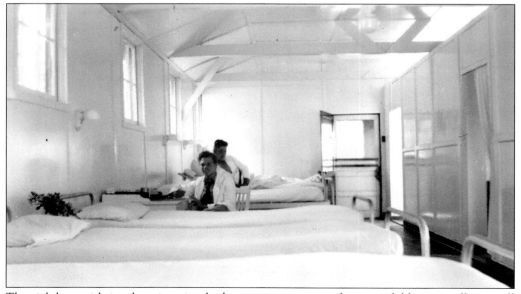

The sick bay, with its clean interior, had separate quarters and was available to enrollees at all times. (Courtesy High Point State Park.)

For many enrollees at High Point, the CCC provided vocational and avocational classes. Academic subjects were taught in local schools. The education program was known as the "School of the Woods" and included job training and current events. Since 45 percent of the men had never been employed and only 13 percent had graduated from high school, this was an important component of the program. (Reprinted from *We Can Take It : A Short Story of the CCC*.)

When the new camp library opened in 1938, it was well equipped and a great source of pride for Company 1280. Many enrollees used the library after work hours. (Courtesy Center for Research Libraries Collection.)

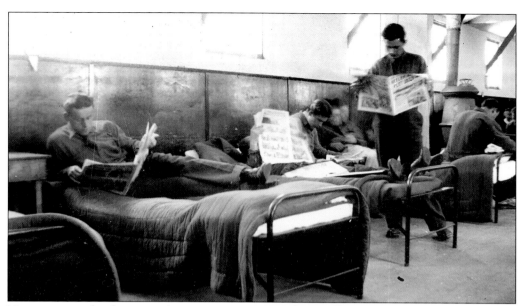

Newspapers and radios were the major news sources for enrollees. Here, enrollees are enjoying their time off in a barracks. The recreation hall provided a place where men could meet and play games like Ping-Pong, pool, and cards. On the night of Orson Welles's radio broadcast called "The War of Worlds," many enrollees thought the broadcast was real and had to be calmed down by camp officials. (Courtesy High Point State Park.)

For camp news, enrollees turned to an in-house newsletter. Both companies had one, although they did not produce them continuously or consistently. This is a cover of one of the few surviving newsletters of Company 216. (Courtesy Center for Research Libraries Collection.)

Current events often captured the CCC boys' interest. When an Eastern Airlines plane piloted by one of the most famous aviators of the day, Dick Merrill, crashed in Matamoras, Pennsylvania, in the 1930s, people flocked to the crash site, including Melvin and Dorothy Gemmill and some of the enrollees. During the World's Fair 1939–1940, a convoy of boys from High Point went to New York to see what the future of the world would be like. (Courtesy High Point State Park.)

Photography was a common hobby in CCC camps across the country. With the introduction of cheap cameras and developing services, many enrollees took photographs during their time at High Point, which now form the basis of what is known about camp life. Enrollee Neil Thiede took this creative picture of the monument at dawn overlooking Lake Marcia in 1938. (Courtesy High Point State Park.)

Boxing and baseball were popular national sports in the 1930s, and most CCC camps, including the one at High Point, had boxing and baseball teams. Enrollees played intra-barracks, subdistrict, and local league baseball games. Company 1280 played for the championship in 1939. (Reprinted from *We Can Take It: A Short Story of the CCC*.)

Sports were a major pastime in camps across the country. Company 1280's successful basketball team was even mentioned in a national CCC newsletter. A camp enrollee made this sketch for the Company 1280 newsletter. (Courtesy Center for Research Libraries Collection.)

The camp's administration occasionally sponsored social events. Here, the mess hall of Company 1280 is decorated for a dance. Notice the arrangements of food on the table in the center of the room. (Courtesy Barbara Sagursky Pohl.)

For most area residents, their memories of CCC boys are of them arriving in the downtown business districts in an army truck similar to the one pictured here. The trucks also were used to transport young ladies to events held at the camp. (Courtesy High Point State Park.)

The administration encouraged boys to put on shows to display their talents. On at least one occasion, girls refused to return to the camp when enrollees complained about their lack of dancing skills. (Reprinted from *We Can Take It: A Short Story of the* CCC.)

Homesickness was a major problem in the CCC, and enrollees were encouraged to write home often. Another problem was enrollees who left their barracks dirty or did not do as they were told. For them, KP (kitchen police) duty was common. (Reprinted from *We Can Take It: A Short Story of the* CCC.)

While in the CCC, the boys often thought of friends, girlfriends, home cooking, and use of the family car (or flivver, as it was then known). Most had never been away from home. (Courtesy Center for Research Libraries Collection.)

The boys wanted to see the girls from Port Jervis and the surrounding area on their time off. Here is a picture of some local young women attending a bridal shower in the early 1940s. From left to right are Mary Innella, Natalie Larow, Julie Pelinski, Katherine Larow, and Zita Innella. (Courtesy Janis Osborne.)

Zita Innella's father forbade her to date CCC boys who came to Port Jervis on their night off. Because they were not from the local area, most parents had no idea from where the boys had come or what their backgrounds were. (Courtesy Janis Osborne.)

Other parents were not so strict, and sometimes a joyful marriage was the result. One CCC wedding was that of enrollee Frank Seddio and Port Jervis girl Fannie Tortorini. Once an enrollee married, he had to leave the Conservation Corps. (Courtesy Janis Osborne.)

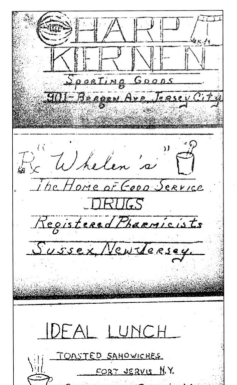

On nights off, one of the pleasures for the older CCC boys was to visit the Port Jervis "foam emporiums," as one newsletter called the local taverns. Local businesses were the beneficiaries of the boys' extra money. When in town, lads occasionally took in a movie, had dinner, and bought sporting goods. (Courtesy Center for Research Libraries Collection.)

Many enrollees still remember the prolific amounts of wildlife in the park, including deer, fish, and elk that the Kusers brought to the park property and enclosed in a fenced area. (Courtesy High Point State Park.)

Many CCC boys came from cities and were not used to seeing farm animals. It was a pleasant surprise for the boundary survey crew when they came across a stray cow from a surrounding farm, as pictured here in August 1937. (Courtesy High Point State Park.)

The seasons at High Point could be difficult to endure because of the extreme weather in that part of the state. This photograph was taken looking southward toward the flagpole, from the center of the row of barracks at Camp Kuser, and shows the result of a heavy snowfall in either 1938 or 1939. (Courtesy High Point State Park.)

No one was excused from snow shoveling duty, including National Park Service foreman Albert Mastriani, who is clearing out the officers' and foreman's quarters. (Courtesy High Point State Park.)

Four

FORESTRY, FIREFIGHTING, AND ROADWORK

When the CCC arrived at High Point, much of the western part of the park, about 8,000 acres, was inaccessible to the public because it lacked passable roads. One of the first priorities of the National Park Service managers was to open up this vast piece of property. In 1933, only 15 percent of the park was accessible. By 1941, most of the park was open to the public. Not only did the CCC create new touring and service roads, but it also created various truck trails, fire lanes, and improved roads used by the local population, including state Route 23 and the Deckertown Turnpike.

As the CCC boys began work in the summer of 1933, they found a forest in bad condition, damaged by disease, fires, ice storms, and lack of maintenance. They cleared the lakebed before the Sawmill Dam was built, continued work already under way at the Steenykill Dam site, and cleared thousands of acres of fallen trees. Their work related to firefighting and prevention saved much forest land. As the years went by, the fires that did occur were less damaging than in the past.

By 1937, when the forestry company was shut down, most of the conservation and forestry projects were completed, and with that, the company's mission was accomplished. The forests within the park boundaries were in good health again. The success of companies like 216 earned the CCC one of its well-known nicknames, "the Roosevelt Tree Army."

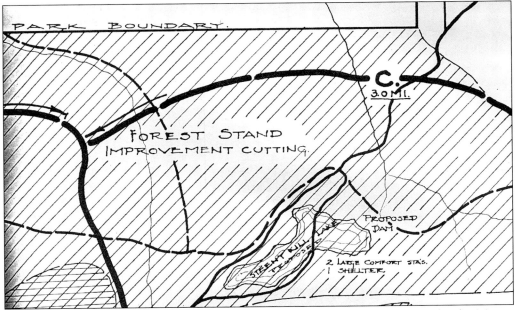

During its first year at High Point, Company 216 cleared forested areas around Lake Marcia and the lake's beach from fire hazards, damaged trees, and low branches. This progress plan, created by National Park Service designers, shows Steenykill Lake, which at that time was only a proposal, along with forest work that was to be done in the northwest corner of the park and around Lake Marcia. (Courtesy High Point State Park.)

The CCC boys were given detailed instructions on how to transplant trees and maintain them properly. Here, five enrollees transplant a large tree at the newly finished Sawmill Dam site. Company 216 planted the entire southern bank with more than 100 trees and several different kinds of perennial plants to create a natural setting. (Courtesy High Point State Park.)

Enrollees dug up and transported trees from within the park to new locations on National Park Service trucks. (Courtesy High Point State Park.)

Enrollees from Company 216 plant trees at the main entrance to the park along state Route 23. In all, about 500 trees were either planted or moved during the CCC era. (Courtesy High Point State Park.)

"Those C.C.C. Guys don't core where They Plant Their Trees, Do They?"

The CCC earned its nickname "the Roosevelt Tree Army" because of the millions of trees it planted. Here, a cartoon from a Company 216 newsletter notes the impact the tree plantings had. (Courtesy Center for Research Libraries Collection.)

CCC boys regularly fought fires not only at High Point but also in the surrounding region. Albert Mastriani drew this fire protection plan for High Point State Park and the surrounding area so that officials would be prepared for any call. Enrollees were regularly given training and fought two or three fires a year on average. (Courtesy High Point State Park.)

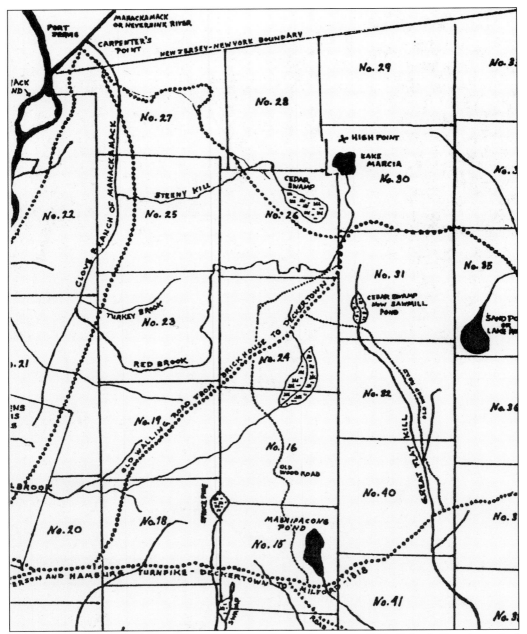

This *c.* 1845 map of the Sussex allotments shows the road system at High Point before the arrival of Col. Anthony Kuser and the CCC. The park is within Lots 16, 24–37, and 40. Steenykill and Sawmill Lakes are shown as cedar swamps. Park Ridge and Sawmill Roads are shown as wood roads. (Reprinted from *High Point of the Blue Mountains*, drawing by Kevin Wright.)

During the early years at High Point, road gangs opened the interior of the park by building or reconstructing old wood roads. After a survey crew laid out the route, road gangs came in to build it. The survey stakes and string for Sawmill Road can be seen. (Courtesy High Point State Park.)

Where previous roads had existed, repair work was fairly easy. Much of the work was done by hand, as CCC boys brought loads of shale and dirt in by wheelbarrows. (Courtesy High Point State Park.)

CCC boys widened this road by filling in the right side with newly harvested stone. (Courtesy High Point State Park.)

In later years, the National Park Service acquired a grader, which is being used here by a CCC enrollee on an old wood road in the western part of the park. (Courtesy High Point State Park.)

In this picture, CCC boys are putting down the final layer of shale to give a newly constructed road a finished surface. (Courtesy High Point State Park.)

After the roadwork was done, enrollees dressed, or finished, the road and its sides. The state would ultimately blacktop it. The CCC built Sawmill Road, Ridge Road, the service access road to Sawmill Lake, fire truck trails, and the Steenykill access roads. In total, the CCC built more than 25 miles of roads in High Point State Park. (Courtesy High Point State Park.)

The roads needed to cross many streams and brooks. For the smaller waterways, a pipe was placed under the road and then finished off with cut stone on both sides. Here, CCC boys are installing a new culvert along either Sawmill Road or Park Ridge Road. (Courtesy High Point State Park.)

For crossing larger brooks, bridges needed to be constructed, requiring a good deal of preparation. This photograph is of an abutment being installed for a bridge that crosses a stream. (Courtesy High Point State Park.)

After the abutment was created, the superstructure was put into place. This is one of the bridges that crossed a culvert on either Sawmill Road or Park Ridge Road. (Courtesy High Point State Park.)

Finally, wood decking and guardrails were installed on the bridges. (Courtesy High Point State Park.)

The CCC boys used dead chestnut trees, which died in the chestnut blight of the 1920s and 1930s, for road construction. Chestnut is resistant to rot and therefore made good guardrails. Here, a work crew builds a guardrail along one of the roads. (Courtesy High Point State Park.)

By 1938, the two companies combined had built more than 8,000 linear feet of guardrails along the roads at High Point. (Courtesy High Point State Park.)

Today, most of the bridge crossings are the result of CCC efforts, although the chestnut guardrails are gone and some of the decking has been replaced. (Courtesy High Point State Park.)

Five

THE BOUNDARY, TRAILS, AND CAMPSITES

When Col. Anthony Kuser acquired High Point, he put together what is thought to have been the most complicated land transaction in the state's history. The subsequent survey of the Kuser donation by the CCC was an important project because it finalized and permanently marked a 40-mile boundary. A survey of a park's boundary was always a priority for the national organization because the government did not want to spend money on private property.

The CCC also built many amenities for campers, including the Sawmill complex. In addition, they helped develop the already existing Appalachian Trail, the Monument and Steenykill Trails, the Sawmill Lake Circular Path, and the Bridle Path (the current Iris Trail). They also designed and constructed ski trails in the eastern part of the park.

The CCC was called on to perform other duties, some off the park premises. On several occasions, they assisted in missing person searches or helped a nearby camp when a fire destroyed some of its facilities. They demolished old buildings that were no longer used and removed miles of wire fencing that had once surrounded Kuser's elk park.

Enrollee Edmund Lauder uses a transit along a park road. Enrollees who worked on surveying projects usually had some mathematical ability. These survey parties took elevation measurements and sited locations, allowing for major projects to proceed. (Courtesy High Point State Park.)

Members of the boundary survey crew work somewhere along the park's border, clearing a line of vision. This was a major project and took several years to complete because of the growth of underbrush and disappearance of landmarks. (Courtesy High Point State Park.)

From left to right, enrollees Alan Wilson, ? Swenson, National Park Service foreman Oliver Wells, and Jack Whittaker take a rest from work on a surveying party with a transit. (Courtesy High Point State Park.)

Oliver Wells, Alan Wilson, and Jack Whittaker work on the boundary survey project while education coordinator David Traub, on the right, observes. Research on the boundary took months to complete. More than 600 deeds had to be examined, many dating back decades. (Courtesy High Point State Park.)

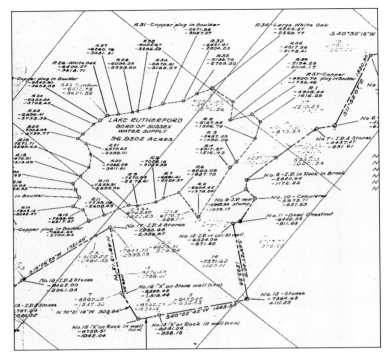

Lake Rutherfurd, a municipal reservoir, was enclosed completely by the park, and monuments were required around the entire boundary. Here, one can see the variety of stations used, including boulders, stones, and trees. (Courtesy High Point State Park.)

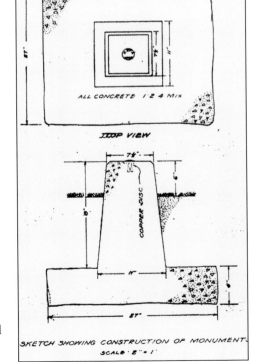

The boundary line was designated by concrete markers like this one, with a bronze dial inserted at the top. Many remain in the park and can still be seen at Lake Rutherfurd beside the Iris Trail. (Courtesy High Point State Park.)

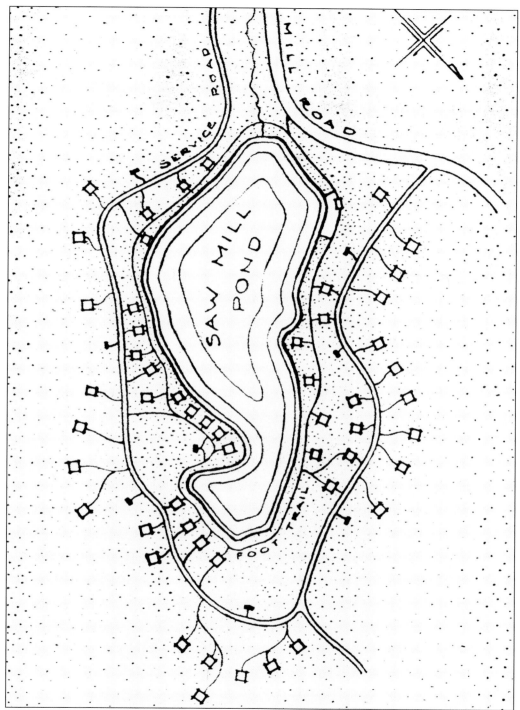

This site plan shows the proposed layout for the Sawmill Lake Campsite Development, which looks the same today except the beach facilities are gone. All of the campsite facilities were built between 1936 and 1939. (Courtesy High Point State Park.)

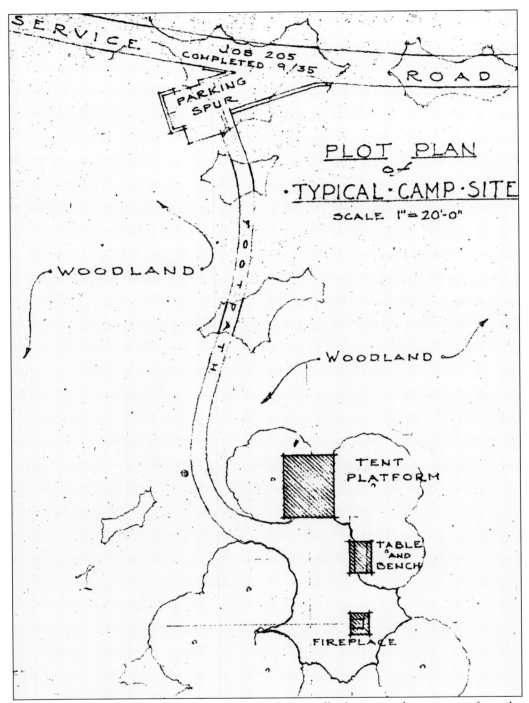

SERVICE JOB 205 COMPLETED 9/35 ROAD

PARKING SPUR

PLOT PLAN
of
·TYPICAL·CAMP·SITE
SCALE 1"=20'-0"

·WOODLAND·

·WOODLAND·

TENT PLATFORM

TABLE AND BENCH

FIREPLACE

Most designs used at High Point were generated internally, but some designs came from the National Park Service Branch of Plans and Design. This plot plan provided foremen and enrollees with a typical campsite layout for use in their construction. Many of the campsites still use this 1930s design. (Courtesy High Point State Park.)

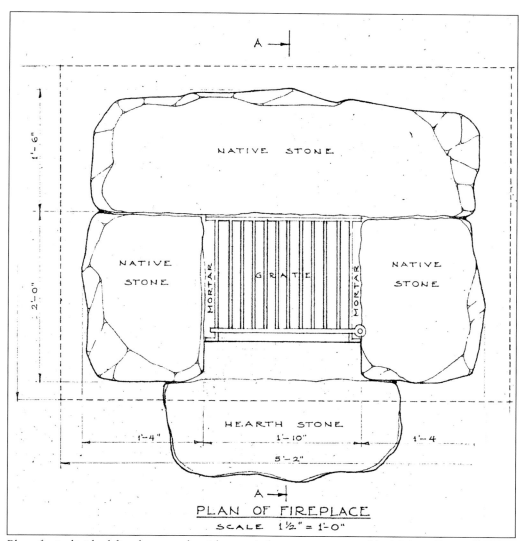

A ⟶

1'-6"

2'-0"

NATIVE STONE

NATIVE
STONE

MORTAR | GRATE | MORTAR

NATIVE
STONE

HEARTH STONE
1'-4"   1'-10"   1'-4
5'-2"

A ⟶

PLAN OF FIREPLACE
SCALE 1½" = 1'-0"

Plans for individual fireplaces made with quarried stone were created by Melvin Gemmill. Also, the old system of providing water to campers through the use of hand-pumped wells, constructed by the Civilian Conservation Corps, has been replaced. However, some of the stone bases remain. (Courtesy High Point State Park.)

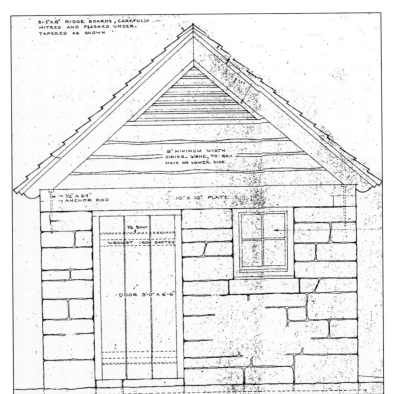

This is an elevation drawing for the comfort station at Sawmill Lake. (Courtesy High Point State Park.)

The comfort stations around Sawmill Lake replaced simple wooden outhouses. Aside from the trail shelters and dams, they provide the park with some of its finest "parkitecture." Here, one of the comfort stations is being built, and stone that would be used in the construction lies scattered around the base of the building. (Courtesy High Point State Park.)

Much of the labor required of the CCC boys was hard and physically demanding. Road building and trail construction throughout the park required moving tons of rock and providing a finished surface. From this hard work came the CCC's motto "We Can Take It!" (Reprinted from *We Can Take It: A Short Story of the CCC*.)

Enrollees Nicholas Hanisak and Carmen Antinello are hiking on the Monument Trail, which was built by CCC work forces in 1940. The photograph was taken by National Park Service foreman Albert Mastriani along with several other photographs that were used in an early park brochure. (Courtesy High Point State Park.)

Among the trail amenities completed by the CCC were three trailside shelters built by Company 216 on the Appalachian Trail. Raymond Torrey, a significant figure in the development of the New York and New Jersey trail systems, said they were among the nicest built in the two-state area. Here is one of them under construction. (Courtesy High Point State Park.)

The concession stand at the base of the High Point Monument was designed by National Park Service foreman Melvin Gemmill and built by park employees. A busy place after it was constructed, it still stands. A subsequent enlargement copied the original design, and so the building is now twice as large as pictured here. (Courtesy High Point State Park.)

The Deer Run Shelter was built in the 1930s and is still used by visitors. It is not clear whether it was built by the CCC or the park. (Courtesy Leslie Crine.)

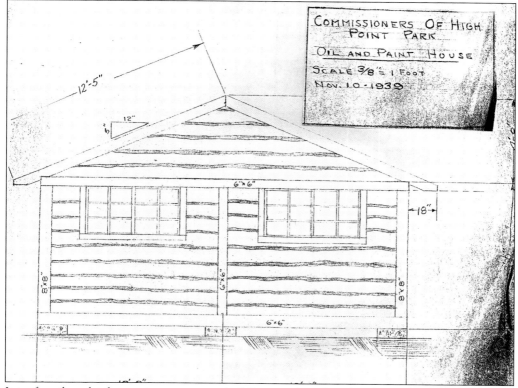

It is often thought that maintenance area buildings, such as the oil and paint house, were built by the CCC, but they were in fact built by the park. While they have the typical rustic appearance usually associated with CCC projects, the plans all bear the signature of the park commissioners. (Courtesy High Point State Park.)

One of the great mysteries at High Point is who built the Iris Inn, now the Visitor Center and Park Office. It is believed, although it is not known for sure, that it was built c. 1940 or 1941 by park forces or a private contractor. It was left vacant for a long time, and while it was commonly thought that the CCC constructed this beautiful building, it is now known that they did not. (Courtesy Leslie Crine.)

This is the interior of the Iris Inn, as it probably looked in 1942. The Iris Inn and the Grey Rock Inn are the most impressive structures in the park. The Iris Inn's interior remains unchanged except for the office area, which was built in the 1970s when it was moved from the Kuser Lodge. (Courtesy High Point State Park.)

Six

LAKES

Among the most complicated projects undertaken by the CCC at High Point was the building of dams that impounded the Big Flatbrook and Steenykill streams. These projects required huge amount of materials, including concrete, stone, fill, and lumber, and demanded constant attention from the boys while the concrete was being made and poured. The dams are among the CCC's most enduring legacies at High Point.

While plans to build two additional lakes were never carried out, the two lakes that were built are still popular features. If the two additional lakes had been built and the Maschipicong Pond property had been acquired, the park would be far different than it is today. There would have been hundreds of additional campsites, allowing for thousands of more visitors.

It is said that Harold Ickes, secretary of interior under Pres. Franklin D. Roosevelt, would not allow artificial lakes to be built in national parks because they would only attract, in his words, "rabid recreation seekers." Instead, hundreds were built in state parks and forests. The lakes remain one of the parks most prized and utilized assets.

Before the CCC built Sawmill Lake, there was a natural cedar swamp that had been dammed and used to power a sawmill built by the Fuller family, a family that has been associated with High Point for decades. The dam, pictured here, was breached at some point, and the new dam was built about 75 feet behind it. (Courtesy High Point State Park.)

The building of the Sawmill Dam required extensive excavations down to suitable bedrock. The first major excavation was for the concrete core of the dam, and the National Park Service power shovel was used to dig deep enough in order to get to the proper level necessary to support the weight of the dam. (Courtesy High Point State Park.)

Large forms had to be constructed to allow for the pouring of the gravity section, which was angled so cut stone could be laid on the downstream side. The pipe pictured in the center of the form is the relief valve, and just behind the form is the sluiceway, which allowed the Big Flatbrook to run unobstructed while construction of the Sawmill Lake dam was completed. (Courtesy High Point State Park.)

Construction of the new dam was undertaken about 75 feet behind the old dam, which can be seen here on the left. Stone from the old dam was probably used in the construction of the new dam. A temporary walkway crossing the Flatbrook was used in the early stages of the project. (Courtesy High Point State Park.)

This view of Sawmill Dam was taken from the lakeside. The creases from the forms that were used can be seen along with a derrick used to lift stone into place on the front of the dam. (Courtesy High Point State Park.)

The entire swamp was cleared of vegetation, dredged, and the material removed. Much of that material was used on the Steenykill Lake project that followed. (Courtesy High Point State Park.)

Probably the most beautifully designed facility at High Point was the Sawmill Lake beach. This drawing was made by Melvin Gemmill and used as a cover for construction drawings for the beach. (Courtesy High Point State Park.)

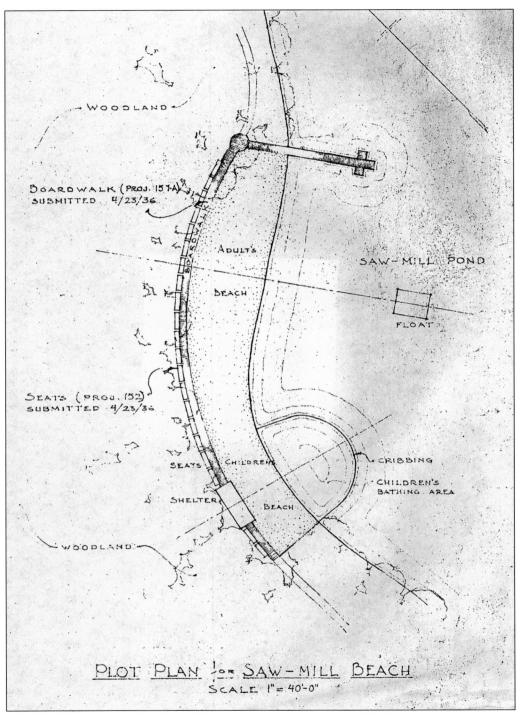

- WOODLAND -

BOARDWALK (PROJ. 157-A)
SUBMITTED 4/23/36

ADULT'S

BEACH

SAW-MILL POND

FLOAT

SEATS (PROJ. 152)
SUBMITTED 4/23/36

SEATS   CHILDREN'S

CRIBBING

CHILDREN'S
BATHING AREA

SHELTER   BEACH

- WOODLAND -

PLOT PLAN for SAW-MILL BEACH
SCALE 1" = 40'-0"

This plot plan shows the Sawmill Lake beach area, including the shelter, boardwalk, and swimming and diving dock and float at the southern end of Sawmill Lake. (Courtesy High Point State Park.)

A construction crew is shown building the boardwalk that encircled the beach. (Courtesy High Point State Park.)

An unidentified National Park Service foreman sits on one of the benches that lined the boardwalk along the beach. (Courtesy High Point State Park.)

A handsome shelter was created at the southern end of the beach, which shaded bathers from the sun. (Courtesy High Point State Park.)

CCC boys level out sand on the beach at Sawmill Lake. (Courtesy High Point State Park.)

A swimming and boating dock and diving board were all built of creosoted lumber, as well as a special pen for the children's bathing area in the shallow part of the lake. (Courtesy High Point State Park.)

Pictured here are campers using the newly opened beach facilities at Sawmill Lake after it was flooded in 1937. The lifeguard stand and diving board are to the right. (Courtesy High Point State Park.)

Shown is the finished dam with National Park Service foreman Albert Mastriani sitting on top of it in 1937. This photograph is typical of the CCC era when enrollees could send photographs to a national developer, in this case the Arrow Photo Service in Minneapolis, Minnesota, who printed them on card stock with a handsome border. (Courtesy High Point State Park.)

Preparation of the Steenykill Lake site and some construction actually had begun in 1931, when the park was acting upon proposals that the Olmsted firm made. It was halted as the Depression deepened in 1932. The construction of the Steenykill Dam was resumed in 1935 by the CCC. It was the largest project undertaken by the CCC at High Point and is said to have been the largest in the state. Here, footers are being created for the concrete core wall of the dam. (Courtesy High Point State Park.)

The progression of necessary forms, including footers and forms for the core wall used for pouring cement, is seen here. In places, the concrete core dam is 45 feet high and 1,200 feet long. (Courtesy High Point State Park.)

A bulldozer on the lake side of Steenykill Dam shows stone riprap being laid, as the large stones are being pushed up the side of the dam and put into place. (Courtesy High Point State Park.)

The only feature of the dam that revealed its original man-made origin was the manhole cover for the blowoff valve installed for use in the event of an emergency. Here, an enrollee tests it. The lake was completed in 1938 and opened to the public in 1939. More recently, work has been completed to strengthen the dam, and so at the present time it has a less natural appearance. (Courtesy High Point State Park.)

These enrollees are either drilling a bore test or working on a relief valve in one of the dams. (Courtesy High Point State Park.)

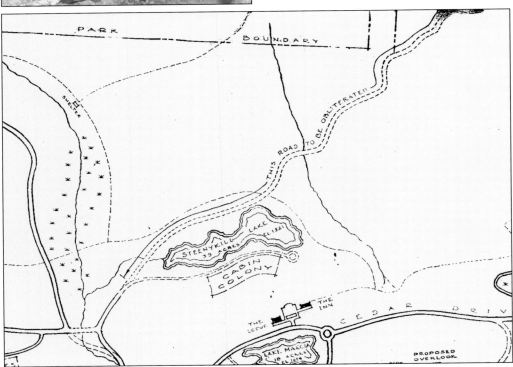

The plans drawn up by the National Park Service called for a colony of 12 cabins to be built at Steenykill Lake. However, only two cabins were built in 1941, both by the park and not the CCC. (Courtesy High Point State Park.)

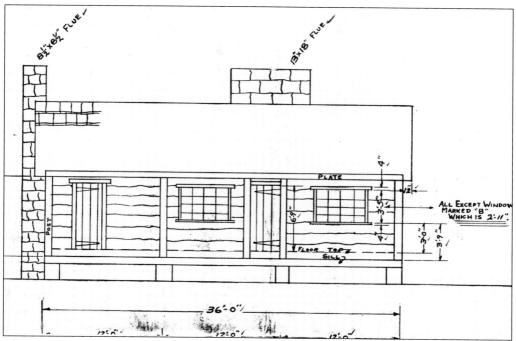

This drawing of a Steenykill cabin was created by a draftsman for the High Point Park Commission and illustrates the popular rustic style of architecture used during the CCC era. (Courtesy High Point State Park.)

The Steenykill cabins remain one of the most used facilities at High Point. Located on the eastern shore of the lake, they are reserved often months in advance. The access road that passes by them is actually former Route 23, which was relocated to its current position when the lake was built. (Courtesy Leslie Crine.)

Enrollees cleaned up about five miles of streams, including the Flatbrook. They also cleaned the stream that runs parallel to Cedar Swamp Road. (Courtesy High Point State Park.)

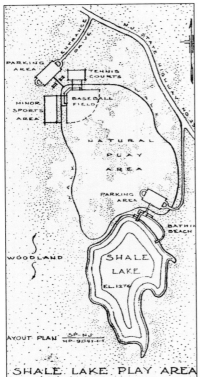

The Shale Lake complex was one of the projects that were not completed due to the start of World War II. Here, just west of Route 23 and south of the present Visitor Center, a large recreational and sports facility with a lake was planned. During the Kuser ownership, there had been on the site a dam, which is still there but is now breached. (Courtesy High Point State Park.)

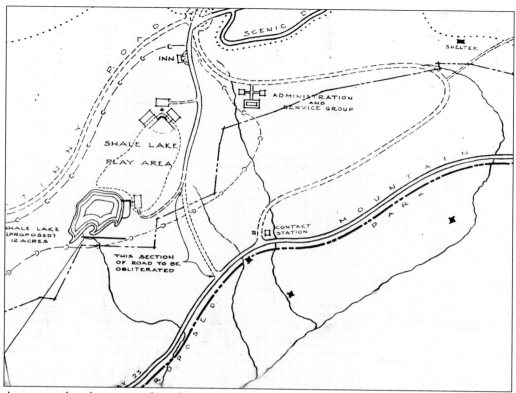

As proposed in the master plan, the area to the east of Shale Lake was to be developed, including administration facilities that were never built. In this drawing, a proposed inn is pictured at the site of the present-day Visitor Center and Park Office. Another possibility that was considered was removing Route 23 entirely and rerouting it along Mountain Road and into New York State to U.S. Route 6. (Courtesy High Point State Park.)

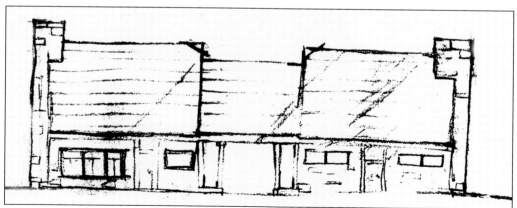

Found among CCC drawings at High Point, this conceptual drawing of what would have been the recreation lodge at the Shale Lake complex is typical of the rustic style used in the period. (Courtesy High Point State Park.)

The parking area for the Shale Lake Play Area was created from a level plateau with an expansive view to the south and east. Here, a crew is working on building the parking lot and finishing off the bank. (Courtesy High Point State Park.)

After the lot was completed, trenches were dug to create a finished parking area with dividers. (Courtesy High Point State Park.)

Here, the parking area is near completion. Much of this work can still be seen today. Beginning in the 1950s, a correctional facility was located here, and inmates used some of the partially completed structures. (Courtesy High Point State Park.)

As part of this large recreational complex, the National Park Service and CCC constructed a ball field, which was still in use as late as 1999, the year the correctional facility closed. (Courtesy High Point State Park.)

A large U-shaped concrete bleacher at home plate was partially completed and used until 1999. It was supposed to have been faced with a bluestone veneer. (Courtesy High Point State Park.)

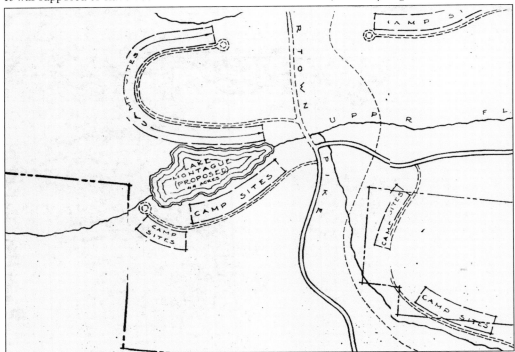

The National Park Service proposed a fourth lake for the park, Lake Montague, south of the junction of Deckertown Turnpike and Sawmill Road. Lake Montague would have been the fourth lake to be constructed by the CCC and probably would have duplicated many of the facilities at Sawmill Lake. (Courtesy High Point State Park.)

Seven

THE CCC BOYS

Almost every one of the CCC boys, now in their late 70s or 80s, remembers how much he loved the triple Cs. Some say they would go back in, if given the chance today. The CCC taught young men about having responsibility for their families at home, being frugal with money, and working hard, while giving them wonderful memories and job skills that many used for the rest of their lives.

A typical CCC boy weighed 147 pounds, was 5 feet 8 inches tall, 19 years old, and served between 9 and 12 months. On average, they had completed eight years of primary school. In the case of High Point, the boys were mainly from urban areas, usually in the northeastern section of the New Jersey. A smaller percentage came from Sussex County or other parts of New Jersey. They received $30 a month, $25 of which they were required to send home to their families. Many of those families had only this income upon which to live.

The long-term benefits the CCC gave not only to High Point but also to the nation are apparent. We still use the parks and forests they built almost 70 years ago, and former CCC enrollees are still proud of that and want to be remembered for their efforts. Hundreds of thousands or perhaps millions of visitors have gone to High Point in the last seven decades, using the roads, lakes, campsites, and trails—all the proud work of the CCC boys.

A typical enrollee, Robert Jackson, stands in front of his barracks in 1937, wearing a full dress uniform. Like the army and National Park Service, the enrollees had their own hierarchy. They were ranked as leaders and assistant leaders. Leaders received $45 per month, and assistant leaders received $36 per month. (Courtesy High Point State Park.)

As many as 2,000 men served at High Point between 1933 and 1941. An average enrollee spent nine months in the CCC, but some men served as long as two years, the maximum length of service. Enrollees that were experienced and rated, or ranked, sometimes stayed longer. These CCC boys pose after working on a culvert along one of the newly constructed park roads. (Courtesy High Point State Park.)

It was not unusual for a cadre of men from High Point to be sent to another new camp to help set it up or assist in some special project. Here, men from High Point are at a camp in Louisiana on a short-term assignment. (Courtesy High Point State Park.)

A cadre from Company 1280 poses before being sent to Company 3219 in Butler in September 1935. From left to right are the following: (front row) Art Walsh, canteen steward; Tom Murphy, first cook; ? Sobeck, infirmary attendant; ? Olino, baker; and ? Bohetz, second cook; (back row) Steve Swetz, mess steward; John Malina, company clerk; Mickey Zagusky, cook; ? Dougherty, second cook; ? Ransteid, assistant education adviser; 1st Sgt. Jim Diamon; and Supply Sgt. Ben Johnson. (Courtesy Barbara Sagursky Pohl.)

Four enrollees stand in front of the barracks housing Company 1280. They are Hilton Babcock, Blackie Railio, John Pinko, and Andy Helancy. The date of the photograph is December 29, 1934. (Courtesy High Point State Park.)

Neil Theide, an avid photographer in his CCC days, took this photograph of half of Barracks 2B in Camp Kuser in February 1937. (Courtesy High Point State Park.)

An enrollee identified only as Mike is pictured in 1937. Most of the young men left the CCC in much better shape than when they arrived. The outdoor life, good food, and hard work made better men of them and in many cases prepared them for an uncertain world that in a few years became embroiled in war. (Courtesy High Point State Park.)

Jack Whittaker of Company 1280 stands outside a barracks building in his long underwear in 1937. Many senior enrollees would initiate rookies by making them do things such as going up to the High Point Monument to wait for an airmail drop. They were told to listen for the plane. After several hours, the rookies would usually come back angry but wiser for the experience. (Courtesy High Point State Park.)

Unnatural trees or unusual natural oddities aroused the curiosity of many boys. Here, enroll-ee Jack Whitaker rides a "horse" somewhere along Sawmill Road in 1937. (Courtesy High Point State Park.)

On his day off, enrollee Alan Wilson enjoys the falls at Lake Rutherfurd in July 1937. The CCC boys took advantage of many of the attractions at the park, including swimming in Lake Marcia, hiking on the Appalachian Trail, and visiting the monument. (Courtesy High Point State Park.)

116

In front of the mess hall, cook
Michael Sagursky is ready to ring
the bell to announce mealtime
for hungry enrollees. (Courtesy
Barbara Sagursky Pohl.)

Michael Sagursky, wearing civilian clothes,
is pictured here in front of an army truck
ready to take the men on their night
off into one of the local communities.
(Courtesy Barbara Sagursky Pohl.)

It is siesta time for some of Company 1280's boys in the back of a National Park Service dump truck in 1936. (Courtesy High Point State Park.)

Members of Company 1280 who had worked on the Sawmill Dam pose for a group picture after their work was finished in 1937. (Courtesy High Point State Park.)

Nicknames were often given to match some feature of an enrollee's personality or job. The sense of camp humor is revealed in this drawing from a March 1938 Company 1280 newsletter. Most of the men pictured had served for at least two years and in some cases, like Tiny Drimmer, had been at the camp for most of its existence. (Courtesy Center for Research Libraries Collection.)

Seven decades have passed since the CCC was created. The young men, such as the one sitting in a barracks building entrance with a camp mascot, are now old men. There is still a light in their eyes when they speak of the CCC and the great adventures they had while serving. (Courtesy High Point State Park.)

Today, the CCC boys are in their late 70s or 80s. Most still remember the CCC with great fondness because it provided them with a job in very difficult times and gave them guidance as they grew into manhood. Niel Thiede, a former enrollee who helped survey the park boundary, sits with his wife, Marie, at their home, located just a few miles from the park. (Courtesy Peter Osborne.)

Eight

THE PARK TODAY

One cannot help but wonder what might have happened if the CCC had operated a few years longer at High Point. There would have been at least two more lakes, and if negotiations had been fruitful, Maschipicong Pond and the proposed Pine Swamp Lake area would have been built. The Shale Lake complex would have accommodated sports activities. Hundreds of additional campsites would have been built along with a number of other trails.

You cannot go into the park without using some CCC-related project. About $1 million was spent in the 1930s for the eight years of work the boys did—a bargain indeed. Across the country, about $3 billion was spent. Many of the projects, such as the roads, lakes, trails, and campgrounds remain, while others, such as the Sawmill Lake Beach Complex and Shale Lake Play Complex, are gone or remain uncompleted. There have been notable losses, including the demolition of the Kuser Lodge and the loss of the Sawmill Lake Beach Complex. With the closure of Camp Kuser, the most ambitious chapter in the park's history was closed, never to be duplicated again.

It is only in recent years that the nation has become interested in the work of the CCC again. While it is unlikely another version of this successful effort could be duplicated, one cannot help but hope that this fine conservation organization might be resurrected in one form or another.

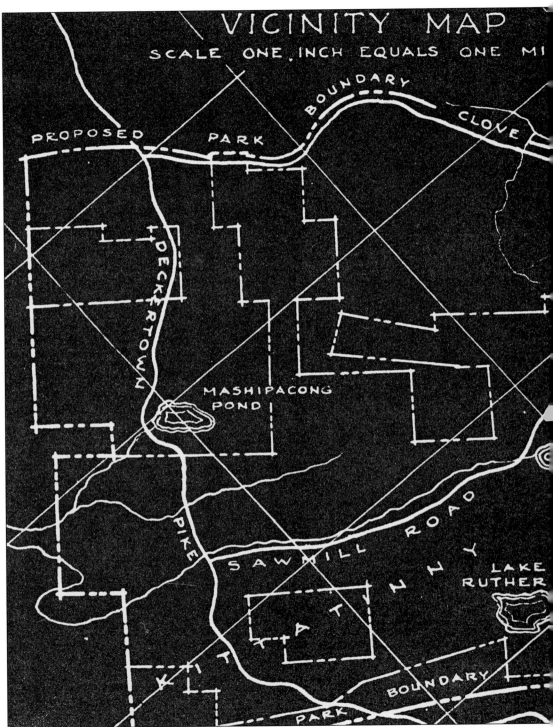

This map shows what the park boundary would have been if the 1938 National Park Service master plan was implemented. The boundaries would have followed the natural lay of the land

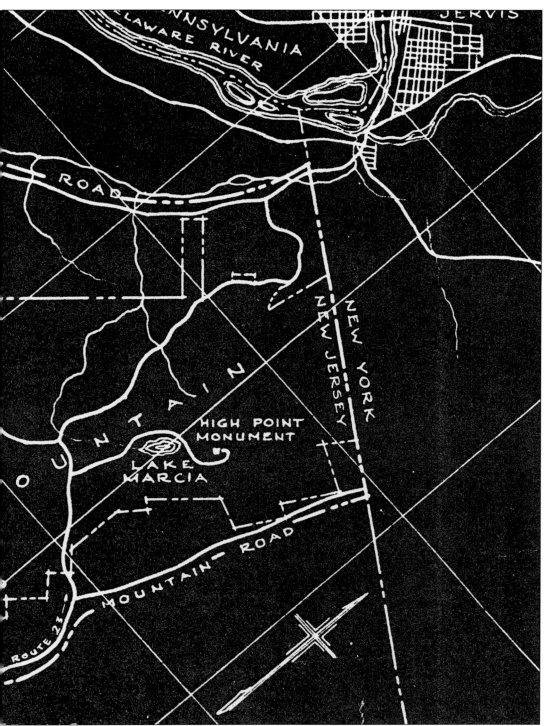

to the Delaware River in the west and not along artificially drawn lines. The park continues to acquire lands, enhancing its territory. (Courtesy High Point State Park.)

The CCC camp at High Point closed in November 1941. Fewer and fewer men were signing up because of the military buildup and draft across America. Within weeks, Pearl Harbor was bombed and America became consumed by the war effort. Here, enlistees leave Port Jervis to join the U.S. armed forces in April 1941. (Courtesy Minisink Valley Historical Society.)

Some 75 percent of the men who served in the CCC would also serve in World War II and were often sought after by military recruiters because of their experience living in a military-style situation. (Courtesy Minisink Valley Historical Society.)

After the rationing, the war bond drives—as shown here in Port Jervis—and the worldwide destruction, the nation wanted to start anew and leave behind the Depression and other memories. Most forgot about the CCC. Nevertheless, Pres. Franklin D. Roosevelt had always hoped that 5,000 camps would be maintained permanently after the war because he thought it such a good program. (Courtesy Minisink Valley Historical Society.)

The biggest project conducted in the park since the CCC days is the Beach Concession building, which is also used to house a cross-country ski center in the winter. It was completed in 1994 and was designed by the architectural firm of Nadasky Kopelson. Its vaulted ceilings and airy feeling are reminiscent of the National Park Service designs, along with its cut stone façade, similar to the Grey Rock Inn. (Courtesy Leslie Crine.)

Only a few traces are left of Camp Kuser, including this stone dock in the picnic area on Cedar Swamp Drive. The camp's buildings were either demolished or sold and reused. (Courtesy Leslie Crine.)

The pavilion at Sawmill burned down in either the late 1960s or 1970s. The ravages of time have taken their toll, and none of the beach facilities still exist. The foundation and stairs are all that remain. Pictured is Jean Crine, wife of the photographer. The Crines have been going to the park since they were children and throughout their married life. Now, they are part of the park's history. (Courtesy Leslie Crine.)

This c. 1960s photograph shows a fire pit with beautifully cut stone built by the CCC. Park employees dismantled the fireplaces in the 1980s and scattered the stones around the campsites to be used as seats around campfires. (Courtesy High Point State Park.)

Just south of High Point is Stokes State Forest, where one of the few memorials in the eastern United States to the CCC stands at the School of Conservation's facilities. This life-sized sculpture memorializes the hard work and dedication of the CCC boys. As we drive on the roads, fish the lakes, and camp in the lovely campsites, we tip our hats to Pres. Franklin D. Roosevelt, who had a vision and acted on it; to the Departments of War, Interior, Labor, and Agriculture; to the National Park Service; to the U.S. Army; and, of course, to the CCC boys, who made it all possible. (Courtesy Leslie Crine.)

BIBLIOGRAPHY

Books

A Guide to Stokes State Forest. Branchville, New Jersey: Stokes State Forest, 1975.

Cohen, Stan. *The Tree Army: A Pictorial History of the Civilian Conservation Corps, 1933–1942,* rev. ed. Missoula, Montana: Pictorial Histories Publishing Company, 1996.

Dupont, Ronald J. Jr., and Kevin Wright. *High Point of the Blue Mountains.* Newton, New Jersey: Sussex County Historical Society, 1990.

High Point Park Commission. *High Point Park: On the Roof of New Jersey.* Newark, New Jersey: the Essex Press, 1928.

Hoyt, Ray. *We Can Take It: A Short Story of the CCC.* New York: American Book Company, 1935.

Honeyman, A. Van Doren, ed. *Northwestern New Jersey: A History of Somerset, Morris, Hunterdon, Warren and Sussex Counties,* Vol. IV. New York: Lewis Historical Publishing Company, 1927.

Merrill, Perry H. *Roosevelt's Forest Army: A History of the Conservation Corps 1933–1942.* Barre, Vermont: Northright Studio Press, 1981.

Osborne, Peter. *We Can Take It! The Roosevelt Tree Army at New Jersey's High Point State Park 1933–1941.* First Books Library, Bloomington, Indiana, 2002.

Quinn, Robert E. *A Brief History of Kamp Henry Kohl 1929–1951,* First Books Library, Bloomington, Indiana, 2002.

Salmond, John A. *The Civilian Conservation Corps, 1933–1942: A New Deal Case Study.* Durham, North Carolina: Duke University Press, 1967.

Wurst, William J. *At the Top of New Jersey: A Brief History of the High Point State Park.* Sussex, New Jersey: Friends of High Point State Park, 1994.

Your CCC: A Handbook for Enrollees. Washington, D.C.: Happy Days Publishing Company, 1940.

Reports and Unpublished Manuscripts

Dupont, Ronald J. Jr. "A History of Mashipacong Pond." 1994.

"High Point: New Jersey's First State Park."

"History of High Point State Park, Sussex County, New Jersey." 1960.

Kuser, Dryden. "Report on High Point State Park, 1958."

"Nomination for Inclusion of High Point State Park on the Register." National Register of Historic Places, Registration Form, Sussex County Historical Society, Newton, New Jersey, 1992.

Olmsted Brothers, Landscape Architects. "High Point Park, New Jersey: A Report Concerning Its Development." Brookline, Massachusetts, 1923.

Osborne, Peter, ed. "We Can Take It: The Roosevelt Tree Army at High Point State Park 1933–1941: Interviews with Former Civilian Conservation Corps Enrollees, Camp Kuser, Companies 216 and 1280," Vol. 1. Rev. ed. 2000.

"We Can Take It: The Roosevelt Tree Army at High Point State Park. 1933–1941: Interviews with Former Civilian Conservation Corps Enrollees, Camp Kuser, Companies 216 and 1280." Vol. 2. Rev. ed. 2000.